Poems For My Younger Phoenix

You are not alone.

Dr Keerthi Elizabeth Jerome

BookLeaf Publishing
India | USA | UK

Made with ❤ on the BookLeaf Publishing Platform
www.bookleafpub.in
www.bookleafpub.com

Dedication

To my mother, Mary Lourde and grandmother, Regeena, the strongest women i knew, phoenixes, in their own right and our guardian angels. Thankyou for guiding and showing me the way.

To my father, K C Jerome, who inspired me to love literature, My husband, Adarsh, who stood by me, through many a storm, and last but not the least, my little sister, Chippy, who brings sunshine, through any rainy day.

Preface

World can be an amalgamation
of chaos and beauty,
and to keep rising from the ashes,
seems to be only way forward..
as life keeps throwing curveballs at you,
my dear younger phoenixes..
my only wish for you..
is to know that,
you are not alone in this battle,
Everything you feel,
all the struggles, hopes and dreams are valid.
I had always penned down
my own thoughts and feelings,
Looking back, I wish,
I could have told my younger self,
that it was okay..
everything will somehow, always find a way.
You will evolve, gradually solve
and finally find your own pace.
Please be forgiving of any mistakes.
I hope this humble collection of my thoughts,
might bring to your life,
solace, acceptance, healing and light.
And most importantly, help you understand,

that you are not alone.

Acknowledgements

Thanking the God Almighty,
The Higher being who always seems to-
guide, care, protect and support,
throughout this labyrinth of life
and manifest in mysterious ways.
I am ever so grateful.
Thankyou.

1. SPARKS

Remember that feeling that sparks inside,
Everytime life tests you and pushes you aside.

That spark..that speaks of an untold anger,
A jeer to the foe, to try push harder.

That tiny spark that wouldn't just die,
No matter how hard you try to bury it alive.

Turn those sparks into mighty flames,
Burn it bright red and change the way of the game.

Even if your path seems hopeless and lame
Even if your feet bleeds amongst the thorn filled lanes

Never loose faith in the power of that tiny spark..
That awaits to be ignited, when the way feels lonely and dark.

Fight back, stand tall along the race..

It is the sparks, that turn into mighty flames.

Remember that feeling, that sparks inside..
Remember your spark and the power of your flames.

2. ALONE IN A CROWD

Amongst the crowd I stay,
Moving downstream along the way.

Suffocated and gasping for breath,
silently draining my own strength.

I tried screaming but my voice was drowned,
I tried fighting..but the efforts never crowned.

Trying to flee from the tide,
But held down by the chains along the ride

Scared by the thousand storms that range inside,
Yet no one else could hear those thunderous sides.

Are all those around me deaf to my silent screams,
Or did they too give up on their once dear dreams.

With no emotions left do they go with the flow?
Or am I a different being to feel so much raw?

When I look around ..I find non like myself..all the masks look alike,
And all the aims the same.

Alone amongst the crowd I stay
Moving downstream along the way.

3. CHOICE

It's all a choice,
Whether to drown or crown..
It's all a choice,
Whether to live or die..
It's all a choice,
Whether your eyes should cry or be dry..
It's all a choice,
Whether you dance or flee..
To the changing rhythms of the life you seek.
It's all a choice,
that can only be made by you.
In this world full of choices, voices and hues,
Never forget,
that you will always have a choice.
Never forget your inner voice.
It's all your choice
and It always will be.

4. I STILL BLOOM

I still bloom,
Even when surrounded by gloom,
Even when crushed by doom,
Even if I will be plucked soon,
Even if I don't receive any boon,
Even if I am surrounded by tombs,
My spot neglected by brooms,
I still bloom,
And dance to sweet tunes,
To spread my subtle perfume,
In a world filled with fake costumes,
I will sing songs to the moon.
And I will still bloom.

5. A REBEL

I have always been a rebel,
And branded so, many a times too,
I embrace the angry falcon
that hisses within me,
that waits to strike back,
At every blow it's been delt with.
I have always been aloof,
To the things that stir on the earth,
While I observe from the sky,
And note the weak points to strike first.
The chains that tried to hold me,
Are drenched with blood,
Both mine and the pitiful chain holder's.
I have always been a rebel,
And branded so, many a times too.
I embrace the angry falcon
that hisses within me,
that waits it's turn, to strike back,
At every blow it's been delt with.

6. THE STALE ROSE

The stale rose, Sighs..
And holds her form,
As long as she can,
Never showing signs,
That you had powers,
Over her, to hurt her.
Never giving you,
the satisfaction of knowing,
Your actions once broke her,
Never showing weakness,
In her thickened darkened petals.
She sighs.. but always holds her form,
Even as her last petal falls..
Graceful, even in dried wrinkled form,
She stands adamant,
Head held high, even in storms.

7. LUST

A four letter word,
that wakes the animal in us.
A four letter word,
that renders the weak willed- insane,
And the strong willed- holy.
A four letter word,
That degrades humanity if uncontrolled
And uplifts love if given with respect.
A four letter word,
Given for the hunger for power, money and flesh..
A simple word,
for the double edged sword we all possess.

8. A KISS

The sealing of lips,
And the deal to secure further bliss.
An Age long tradition,
To express ones passion and affection.
A window of transition,
From friendship to love completion.
An erotic sensation,
That often leads to addiction.
The gateway to start a relation,
Gotten after much negation.
An unearthly intoxication,
That drive men wild with anticipation.

9. VULNERABLE

An open book,
That's easy to tear and smear,
open and prone,
to its contents being,
torn and ripped,
it never easy to be an open,
vulnerable little book.
Letting out all the feelings,
And not bottling up any away,
Wearing the heart on your sleeve,
Easy to pluck and easier to crush,
Vulnerability and transparency
are difficult choices,
In this world full of people,
looking for new ways to chagrin the heart.
Yet being vulnerable
has a beauty that's sublime and true.
Against the backdrop of fake smiles
It shines with its own rare light.
Being true to oneself,

Is in itself, the greatest prize.
For in the long run
we need no one to prove but ourselves
Of all the transparent passions emotions and scars
that transpired across this brief journey called life.

10. LOOK INTO MY EYES

Look into my eyes,
And tell me what you see,
Is it the fire that burns,
With a passionate blaze,
Deep within my core?
Or is it the ice that chills
the air to frost,
Filled with indignation and ghosts?
Or is it the spring of love,
Filled with tender roses and cloves?
Or the sadness that enclaves,
the rocky ocean floors.
What do you see?
And what do you feel?
Through these windows of mind,
So subtly called as the eyes of mine.
Do, please look deep,
and tell me what you see.

11. TEACH YOURSELF

That it is okay to cry,
that it is okay to blunder,
that imperfection are fine,
that self love is a wonder,
that skills are self taught,
that expectations can hurt,
that gratitude always gains,
that only you can hold your reins,
that you are your own greatest friend,
as well as your deadliest enemy.
Teach yourself to improve,
at every stage of life's game.

12. PAINFUL TRUTHS

I swallow truths,
the painful revelations,
the hard realizations,
the truths that stings my eye,
the demons that chase,
My peace of mind..
Just so that I wont disturb,
The tranquillity of my dear ones.
So that they won't shed the tears,
Their peace is my price..
For all the hard bitter truths I hide.

13. SANCTUARY

You asked me,
To take your hand,
And run away to the beautiful hills,
A sanctuary for tired souls like us,
With evergreen trees,
And blissful cool winds,
Snow covered hills and sweet streams,
Wildflowers and a warm wooden home,
Night filled with enigmatic stars,
And the cold weather that prompts hugs.
To a beautiful dream you beckoned me,
Reaching out your firm hands,
Away from the toils of dreading lives,
Away from the suffocating watchful eyes.
You asked me,
To take your hand,
And run away with you, to the hills.

14. LOVE IS A FEATHER

Let it float around,
Dont hold on too tight,
And crumble its form..
Dont take it too much for granted,
And let it fly far away,
Losing its sight forever..
Observe its delicate structure,
And take pride in its sublime nature,
And acknowledge its presence,
While it floats around..
Relish its beauty..
In its free and untainted form..
Let its presence lighten the soul..
In its free unbridled form.
Let love fly..
Like a feather in a light breeze..
In its true form.

15. LETTING GO

The realization..
that I didn't truly matter to them,
that I lived in a sheltered bubble house ,
Made from my own illusions..
A dream of fantasies,
that I wanted to be true.
So far away from the reality,
that I tried hard to blissfully ignore..
Hoping, my daydreams were the truth.
The truth however was
like a icy cold wave,
that scattered my bubble house,
against the hard rocks on the rugged shores.
The final decision to let them go,
Was to give my mind a break..
From spinning stories to redeem them..
Excuse their behavior..
And continue to pretend,
everything was fine.
Letting them go..

Was to, Put down the weights,
Realize the truth,
And figure out who is worth suffering for..
Who holds you dear and who holds you hostage..
Who values you and who is using you..
While finding the strength to walk away,
Heartbroken but head held high,
Was where I found the beauty of letting go.

16. GREY

Between black and white,
There's a grey zone..
Where nothing
Is pure black nor white
In its true form..
The light and darkness merge..
The right and wrong interlink,
Happiness and sadness co exist,
And moral judgements of men
Stands confused in the abyss
that unfolds within..
Aren't we all a part of the grey zone..
Where right and wrong
Truth and lies
Assumptions and realities
Black and white
Intercalate to amalgamate
into a grey zone..

17. A WITCH

A witch, they called her,
She lured their men and husbands
with her charming ways and spells,
She dared to read the books,
That were handled by men,
They feared she would open another universe,
She dared to ask questions,
Of traditions old, new and worn,
She dared to fight back
and use her voice,
When she was expected,
to be meek, mute and calm,
She dared to follow her heart
in work and love,
She dared to disgrace their pride,
in the name of lust and love.
Lust was meant for only men,
how dare she sin?!!
They burned her and the likes of her,
at the stakes where she screamed,

They drowned her in rivers
so her voice and queries will dim,
In the name of witch hunt,
wounded egos and lies profound,
They hunted her down,
and let the likes, of her end.
But the seeds were already sown.
Crying against the injustice,
A thousand new witches,
were born from stumps unknown.
More books were read,
and more chains broken and thrown,

18. DEATH OF SOMEONE WE LOVE..

When everyone seems to be moving ahead
You stand still and watch..
Wondering if you have really felt the pain ,
To get over it so soon?
You wait, wait, wait and wait..
For the pain to crush you down..
You wait for the moment when,
You realise that they are really gone..
All these days, you smiled and thought,
"I can do this alone"
But the truth lies in the fact that
Once they are gone, you always be alone..
Each leaf of a growing tree,
Might one day fall apart..
Each making its own path,
Across the lines of time.
Each memory softly printed,
Upon some vague matrix inside you,
Plays their harps as long as you survive..

Urging you to move on with your life,
And to leave them locked,
Forever safe
In the corner of your heart ..
Forever safe in the corner of your heart..

19. FACING FEARS

One day or another
My dear trembling heart
You need to face your battle..
That life throws around the corner
Be it, broken heart or broken life
Fear of heights or fear of sea
Fearing losing the one you love
Or the fear of being ordinary
One day or another
My dear trembling heart
You need to face your battle..
For life will keep on throwing you
The same set of tests
Until one day you conquer them
And set yourself free.

20. THOUGHTS AND INK

When my thoughts overflow,
I let them flow,
In the form of ink,
that merges into images,
Of my soul.. onto papers,
Spread on the floor.
Trying my best,
to make them imprint,
The essence of my feelings,
Emotions, merits and flaws,
To let the papers soak up,
The thoughts and a part of my soul,
And reflect the essence,
Back to me,
like a mirror unflawed.

21. HEALING

I searched for my healing far and wide,
For the sponge that can wipe,
the stains and scars from my soul,
Far and wide I searched for the cure,
In books, poems, temples and travels,
I searched for the meaning of my life,
A magic potion to cure my soul,
And heal me and my broken form..
Like a wanderer lost in the desert sands..
looking for the answers that seems lost in time.
The rush that seemed to engulf me,
Suffocating and smoldering me,
Suddenly disappeared into thin air,
During my brief encounter,
with the serene being inside me - myself.
The answers were inside me all along..
Just close your eyes and listen to its call.
I was on a ruthless march
to conquer worlds and mountains,
Without once trying to gain myself, as an ally.

The peace I feel during the troublesome day,
After leaving the difficult tasks
the Infinite Providence that helps us
day and night,
Is as sublime as the gradual, steady
and graceful blooming of a rose,
among the thorns,
with its own true cherished form and scent,
Without losing its identity in this troubled world.

22. IN A CAGE..

I feel like I am living in a cage,
made from my insecurities, despire and rage,
All the voices that tells me what to do,
All the scrutiny and things to prove..
Suffocates me silently in my sleep
And makes me yearn for any break however meek..

I miss how I used to soar the moors,
how I stretched my wings and touched the moon..
I played with the stars and howled with the wolves..
Yet here I am unable to move.

I beat against the iron rods of my cage,
I squirm under the hatred of my gate,
That sees, my longing for freedom as a deadly sin..
For I am provided with all the necessities for life to begin,
And my longing to be free is an absurd thing..
For the cage is golden and there are plenty of swings.

Yet I long to fly freely between the mountain passes..
Free from this golden prison and it's clauses..
For at least a moment ,alas..
Free from this suffocating bass..
I know that I am living in my own cage.

23. HOPE FROM A DEW DROP

Every early morning dew drop
Brings in me, a surge of new hope.

With a tiny sun sparkling inside,
Setting the memories of the dark clouds, aside.

Conquering territories, one at a time,
Welcoming the new day with a smile so sublime.

Warmed by a fire, shinning bright in its heart,
Reflecting the heavenly light, guiding it through the leafy path.

I will bloom one day,
Like these flowers of May.

Soar the open skies,that have no limits or bays,
Be like the birds of paradise throughout my days.

Fly above the rain and thundering storms,
Conquer the deep valleys and adversaries of all forms

Letting the light inside sparkle brighter and strong,
Like a thousand dew drops in a field after a storm.

Facing the bright horizons and the new born sun,
Reflecting hopes and dreams of days filled with fun

24. THE NIGHT SKY

Through a dark moonless night,
The thousand jewels of night time sky
Shines sweetly in the infinite sky.
The fragrance of the white flowers
Drafts through the air, so deliquescently light.
The snowy hills shine pearly white
Against the darkest hour of the night.
The deep pools reflects the heaven above
Filled with white dwarfs, black holes
and mighty red giants of long ago.
So huge to even meet the eyes,
Yet they humble themselves to tiny sparks
Winking during the night time,
Lulling and luring one to sound sleep,
Telling everyone that, it will be fine.
Smiling slowly and fading out
Accompanying us till the end of dark.

25. THE SILENT PAIRS OF EYES

Both of them knows, that their eyes want to meet,
Even when molten in ego and hate...
When one stares, the other looks away,
Hiding behind the mountain high pride.
Sorrow, shame and a tinge of regret,
Shades and shadows those silent eyes,
As they wander about,
Staring at anything except,
Those pair of reproachful eyes,
That watch from a distance, so far away,
Like a tiger, waiting for it's prey...
But the gazelle avoids it's well laid trap
And Silently walks away,
Hoping never to meet those lustreless eyes,
That speaks only of wounded pride.
Both of them knows, that their eyes want to meet,
Even when molten in ego and hate...
Once upon a time,they had met..
But never will they meet again...

26. FROZEN LANDS

I miss you, my friend,
Like the summers and the golden skies,
In this frozen barren lands.
Amongst these frozen thorny barks,
I wander about, bleeding from my gaping wounds,
Dragging my tired little blood stained feet along,
In search for what I have long lost..
Oh! How I wish you were near, my friend..
For you would never let me shed a tear,
And help me walk through my fears..
Your smile could sprout spring in snow,
Our laughter made the summers glow,
It was the little things that made our days..
Oh! Why did fate let us part in our ways?!
I miss you, my friend,
Like the summers and the golden skies..
In this dry frozen barren lands.

27. MY FIRST REAL CRUSH...

There you were,
Standing tall and straight,
Looking ahead with an intense gaze,
That made me feel,so out of place.
You walked with confidence,
You talked with care..
Little did I know, that,
It would be your face and name,
That I saw everywhere,
for the rest of the days..
I often wondered 'why you..?'
You were just another silly boy!
I have seen many like you,
Yet dint feel my heart beat this way.
The happiness I felt beside you,
Made my pains go away.
My heart broke, when I heard you were sad..
It leapt with joy when you were glad.
Yet, each time I talked to you,

You simply jeered and moved away.
Each time, I resolved to let my feelings fade away..
To look away when I see you,
Since you never really cared,
Nor gave a second thought..
To this 'just an ordinary' girl,
With a silent pair of lips,
That never spoke their intended words.
Sometimes I wonder, if you knew I existed,
Or you knew all along and chose to ignore it..
All I know for certain is that..
You were my first real crush...

28. THE IMPASSE

When I can't see, nor hear,nor understand,
When I stand on the way all alone,
When I finally understand who all are true,
When I feel done for, hopeless and stricken down

I stay.. and try to catch my tears
And the brimming sorrow that floods my senses

I wanted to fly, but here I am
Bleeding from my broken bones and shattered wings
The wounds gap wide, leaving my heart restless
The sorrows stab deep when the unending guilt screams
out my name,
While I stand ashore, alone,tired and too proud to weep

Hiding the sorrows in a well built mask
That lets only laughter and glad things pass outside
Fighting the despire that keeps trying to drown me
Every step I take leaves my feet bleeding..

Yet I need to walk, I need to keep moving,
As long as I breath I won't stop trying.
Step by step I need to heal my broken wings
Stretch them wider, make them stronger
Arm them to cover whole new horizons,
Prove myself with those broken and healed dreams

In this plain dark land,
I found myself.. what I am and who I am.
I thank the wounds that drained away weak blood
The pain that reminded me of my mortal self
The despire that let me notice the faint shades of joy

29. MISUNDERSTANDINGS

Difference in tone of voice,
Can be the source of all this noise.
Ideas conveyed can be differently perceived,
And the love intended inside, never received..
All because, our mind jumps to conclusions,
And believes firmly in hurtful delusions.
Yet, spending a little time with the facts alone..
Can set the things right back along.
Five minutes of patient ranting,
Can save both hearts, from sorrow and anger pending.
It makes the world a better place..
And heart a beautiful, joyful and peaceful space.

30. THE THIN LINE INBETWEEN..

There is a thin line between,
Insanity and genius,
Need and greed,
Love and lust,
Innocence and stupidity,
Customs and superstition,
Patience and exasperation,
Smartness and manipulation,
Loneliness and solitude,
Deadlines and targets...
And everyday things we ought to do.
But it's we who decide where the line stands,
And it's we who decide it's thickness and its strength..
In everything we do,
There's always a thin line in between two..

31. THE STRONGEST ONES..

The strongest ones,
are those who hide their sorrows
behind their laughs,
for they know the power of humour
and how it lightens the clouds..
if you look closely,
Only the intensity behind their eyes,
gives away any clue-
to their true profile,
the long past that built them
and the constant fire
burning in their hearts.

32. THE WAVES OF SILENCE

Thinking about life,
Its ups and downs,
It's mad rush and dreaded hours.
Alone, in meditation,
All these thoughts comes,
Rushing around.
As each thought is hushed ,
The other arises.
Outside it appears calm,
Yet inside me there is an active storm.
Silent to the outside world.
Waves of thoughts arise in my head,
And lashes across my sandy banks.
Silent to the world,
The waves always arise,
One by one..by one.
Even when I am silent and calm.

33. TRAVELS

The farther I go,
The deeper I unearth,
Myself, my desires
and my dreams.
The farther I went..
The more I discovered,
My limits, my hopes
and my wings.

34. TEARS

The clear elixir that flows
From my eyes
Every time my heart breaks
And I feel a suffocating pain ..
I wish I could take back.
To tell myself not to be this fragile.
To shake myself and tell me to stop.
The endless involuntary tears
That swell up in my eyes,
Due to actions that was not mine,
For others carelessness and arrogance,
Their indifference and ignorance,
Why should I waste my tears..
Yet each night the clear elixir,
still flows from my eyes..

35. YOUR HAIR REMINDS ME OF..

The stages and steps in your life,
There was a time, u braided it long,
To please your parents,
to adhere society's norms.
The good girl at home.
Then came a teenager with shy eyes,
Who valued boys attention,
And wanted to win attraction,
By various crops, fringes and styles.
The first love, where u took extra care,
For the hair to glow and be soft.
The heartbreaks that left your hair
Uncared for, messy in drought.
The resurrections and transformations
That made you colour your hair
and make it further short..
Lastly the self exceptance,
that made you choose your style.
And learn your plot.

Your hair reminds me of your story,
the journey you have come through..
It truly is a crown of glory,
for all the things,
you have gone through.

36. THE NIGHT IS LIKE A RIDDLE

That awaits to be solved,
Pieces by pieces,
Bit by bit, amongst the black holes.
The millions of stars,
Lays themselves bare,
Exposing their mysteries,
Yet protecting their secrets from afar.
The constellations dance,
Hiding futures and pasts,
Before men's naked eyes.
Night is a like a riddle,
That awaits to be solved.

37. WILL YOU BE MINE?

In sickness and health,
Hand in hand for life,
To share my joys and my sorrows,
To rest my head on your shoulders,
To talk in the language of poetry,
To joke around and lighten miseries..
Will you be mine..
To hold and cherish till death we part.
To share the adventures
And to talk our hearts out..
To cherish and tolerate
each others credits and quarks,
To fall asleep in peace in each others arms..
It's a simple question..
that deserves to be asked,
Will you be mine?
So my days on earth
is spent with you by my side?
In sickness and health,

Joys and sorrows,
Till death do us part.

38. THERE'S NO GUARANTEE..

There's no guarantee
That we will be happy and free,
Flying like birds of paradise,
Among the shady palm trees..
Every now and then,
I doubt our durability..
For we are like matchsticks,
That waits to start,
a forest fire amongst the brittle dry leaves.
You and I are as different,
as opposite poles of the magnets can be..
Becoming too familiar and similar,
In the long run, seems,
to repel us, as we proceed..
There's no guarantee..
That we will be happy and free,
Yet the sense of adventure,
Beckons us to meet..

39. LOVE IS THE LONGING..

For someone to make you whole,
For someone to share your joys,
And hug you when in sorrow,
For someone to share your stories with,
To gaze upon their love filled eyes,
and listen to them sing sweet love songs.
To walk out the door everyday,
knowing they will guard you with their life.
To listen to their adventures,
And make trips that leave memories for ages,
To hold each others hands,
And walk in meaningful silences.
Love is an eternal longing,
To be cherished , treasured and felt
From deep inside our soul.

40. I CHOOSE YOU

I choose you,
Amid the storms and the blues,
Because I saw a light in you,
flickering in the darkness.
the darkness that tried to blacken,
and swallow your path,
Yet your fire and light blazed strong and freed you,
From its gnarly claws,
I saw how you fought,
With tooth and nail,
Against the darkness that intended,
To defeat you..
I fell in love with the warrior you are,
Who fought battles that noone else knew,
I watched in awe,
As you fought your battles one by one
and won,
I have seen your fire blaze high..
burning up dark abodes..
That was what inspired me,

To choose you as mine.
And I am happy, dear warrior,
That I chose you.

41. DESTINY IS A PAINTING..

Full of vivid colours and days,
Dark and gloomy backgrounds,
And startling hues ,
Intermix and twirl around,
In this canvas called life.
Some so gloomy that
the heart turns black,
Others so bright, the eyes blind.
The blood lust red,
And serene greens,
The joyous yellows,
And tranquil blues..
Life turns around and uses all its hues.
Till the end of the painting..
The canvas shows.
The journey of colours,
That lined the destiny,
Like a beautiful painting,

That from the beginning,
Had so much meaning.

42. IF I WERE A STATUE

I would feel no pain,
And not be branded,
As a sensitive soul.
I wouldn't get involved,
In things I can't control.
I would watch silently,
From the sidelines,
And feel no remorse.
I would let people pass by,
And never want to talk.
I would be inert to the stress,
And numerous strains of the world.
I would be a silent watcher,
With no emotions to control,
No mind to read,
no heart to feel,
And icy stone cold.

43. ON SILENT NIGHTS..

I wonder if you miss me,
Or have you fallen asleep already?
If you are as restless
and agitated like me?
Tossing and turning,
With a broken heart
And silent tearful screams.
Or have you fallen asleep already.
Me forgotten like an old dream.
That washed ashore by fate,
Stayed a little while
And slowly drifted away
In another tide of the sea..
Never even creating a ripple,
In your tempest , of a mind,
A silent lotus that was tainted,
In your garbage spewn sea.

44. WHEN YOUR SCARS SHINE..

They light up your whole world,
Like beacons that lead the way,
To the ultimate destiny.
For every scar cracks open,
Your heart, making thy
light shine through,
Spreading it to the world around you,
In the form of compassion,
love and empathy.

45. THORNS

I think..
She built up her thorns,
As a defence..one by one,
For each heartache, pain and scorn
She had received on the way to her glory,
So that non will dare to pluck her again,
As she blooms into a queen flower,
In the grandest peak of her
ever evolving story.

46. CALL ME A MERMAID..

Call me a mermaid,
For I am creature in love
with my passionate sea,
It's waves are a part of me,
It's mystery magnifies my allure..
Tempting sailors to the abyss,
As I sit feigning innocence and serenity,
amongst the jaggerd rocks,
Giving them hope,
letting them race towards me,
So I can watch from a distance,
as they drown and die,
In my mystical sea of love ..
While I pretend to sigh..
Call me a mermaid,
For I am a creature in Love's sea,
That drowns it's hunters,
in pursuit of lust.
While I watch calmly,

from the jaggerd unforgiving rocks,
amongst the deep sea.

47. WHEN THE NIGHT HOWLS..

my heart and soul howls too,
At the moon , in long vengeful cries,
Expressing my happiness, sorrows,anger and lust.
In an ancient language filled with passion,
I howl my heart out to the moon,
Expressing my repressed feelings,
And getting the weight out my soul,
I howl and speak to the moon,
One with the nature and tune,
When the night howls,
My heart and soul howls too,
Due to Awakening of the ancient being,
Trapped for now , in this bodysuit,
Who is one with the nature, creatures, earth's soil and soul.

48. WHEN FLOWERS WITHER..

When flowers wither,
They are still content,
Happy to have lived a life,
So full of joy, sorrows, lovers and peace.
They are not jealous ,
of the younger blooms.
Their reminiscence of past is bitter sweet.
The bees that were their lovers,
Are bade a sad kiss,
To the friendly breeze,
They gently swing.
Happy to be alive,
a pure spirit, gentle and sublime,
They wither without complaints,
And gently drops their petals,
in graceful strides.
And slowly faints away
Ever sweet, beautiful and quiet.

When flowers wither,
It's still a graceful sight.

49. THE NUMBNESS

That seems to engulf me,
From which I try to desperately,
Break free..
Like weeds that creep in my garden,
Strangling me slowly,
Like quicksand that devours me,
Eating me alive as I struggle to be free..
My only salvation is to be still and feel,
Accept my realities and breath slowly..
Stop waiting for the numbness to recede.
Immerse myself into the cloud fully..
Hoping that once I feel every sorrow deeply..
I might one day break free.
As a scarred but stronger human being.

50. TELL ME HOW TO BE FREE..

Tell me how to be free,
Like the wind, rain and sea,
That answers to noone,
Whose happiness is not tied to anyone,
They soar so carefree,
Untied to the responsibilities,
Tell me how to be free.

51. DANCE

The eternal rhythm,
that flows through my veins,
Comes alive in ecstasy,
When I sway to the songs men sing.
The joy is boundless,
As I tune in on the beats,
And plays music with my body and soul.
Letting the sounds drench me
from head to toe,
Letting the music bring peace to my soul,
As I dance to these beats,
Let my body be my witness,
On how powerfully it sways my core.
And how each beat,
Magnifies my essence and eternal rhythm,
That flows , breaths and live in my veins and soul.

52. FED UP OF HIDING FROM..

My own true self,
In its fullest splendor and form,
For the fear of what,
The society might think and say.
Curbing the urges to speak aloud,
About my passions, dreams and woes,
To receive enriching love,
And to speak my mind,
Amongst the stereotypical way of life..
Fed up of hiding myself,
down the ditch.
Negating who I really am..
Covering up the perfect flaws,
And being an ideal candidate.
Fed up of hiding,
My own true self,
In its fullest naked splendor and raw form,
For the fear of what,
The society might think and say.

Hiding, to maintain an imaginary world,
Where everyone secretly wishes for,
The perfectly normalized imperfections,
And a mind that's sane.

53. MISTAKES..

Why do I keep..
Repeating the same mistakes,
Thinking, things have changed..
When infact..
I am as naive as always..
Masked under the false pretence,
Of having learned from my past mistakes,
By undergoing the long trials and tribulations
And its consequence on the way.
I repeat the same mistake,
Now clothed in another embodiment,
In another time and place..
Making me wonder,
If I am a slow learner or do I not learn at all..
About truths regarding trust, love,
loyalty, manipulations, betrayals and war.
Why do I make the same mistakes,
In different forms and ways.

54. IDENTITY

The entity which we all..
aspire, strive and envisualize to achieve.
The concept of ourselves in our mind,
That guides our actions, behaviours and patterns..
culminating in our efforts..
To uphold the ideas of our own identity..
Firmly believing in our ability to metamorphosis, evolve and better ourselves..
From our previous state..
We all silently race to define our identity.

55. I USED LOVE..

As an means to escape my reality,
To forget my insecurities,
To cushion the downfalls..
Only to realize..
That those unhealed wounds
Will always bounce back..
At the next opportune moment,
If not healed completely..
And love is never an antidote,
That can be used to escape reality.

56. THE PRACTICAL ONE..

So brute and sharp,
Like the cold butchers knife,
It cuts through the meat,
Let the vessels bleed,
So focused on the outcome,
Impartial to the meat's wince,
From the pain along,
The cold metals path.

57. TO BE AN ANGEL

I tried..
Sacrificing my needs,
To cater to the wants of those alive,
Letting my wounds bleed agape while,
I nursed the rest of them
back to life..
To be an angel,
I tried..
I let myself be drowned,
For others to thrive..
Yet I still can't figure out..
If trying to be an angel,
Is my weakness of foolish pride,
Or is it a blessing sublime.

58. FEAR OF LOSING MYSELF, FOR YOU..

Losing my sense of self and identity,
Sacrificing myself to fit your small world,
Of denying my feelings and emotions,
Of thoughts that tend to be interpreted,
As something else entirely new..
Of emotions that are blunted by
Your brute reality sense and practicality,
Of living in a cage,..
Alone with myself and you as a shadow presence..
That doesn't really care if I stay or leave.
I fear losing myself
while trying to accommodate..
You into my life..
It's like I have to blunt my emotions
and ignore my thoughts..
Say only happy things..
listen to your monologue
while my thoughts and emotions
has to be silently buried inside me.

And I burn from inside..
Please don't ask me to choose you..
For I will have to loose myself and
sacrifice my individuality to choose you.

59. YOUR ORGINALITY..

We search for perfection..
Has mental pictures of how it presents,
Drowning ourselves in its attainment..
Only to realise ...
How many masks we were wearing to fit in..
Looking around.. Everyone wears the same.
And runs the same rat race.
So scared of judgements ...
If we are silly, moody or serene..
In a world where everyone wears masks,
To fit into the mould of our own minds making.
Let it go.. the masks and the facades,
Unearth your true self,
From deep within you..
And let your original light shine through.
Because, that mould you hold onto..
Is just an illusion of control.
Like a mighty elephant who thinks,
He's tethered to a small thin peg and rope.

60. I PAINT MY SCARS..

With brilliant hues,
Designed to distract the viewer,
From the depth of my wounds,
To let my scars lay hidden,
From the prying eyes..
So that my wounds will heal
in peace and away from suffocating lies,
I paint my scars with brilliant glistening hues..

61. IN YOUR EYES..

I saw my reflection
in your glistening black depths,
Looking prettier than I actually was,
For it was tinted with your love for me,
That burned and hide my flaws, away..
While your eye smiled at me..
So affectionately.. In its sublime light.

62. PAIN

I truly believe
That the crushing the heart,
Makes the poetry flow,
Its scars run deep
And tears that turn to streams..
Awakens the beautiful poetry,
That lies hidden inside deep..
As a means to unburden the heavy load..
Poetry ,creativity and prose,
freely flow , trying to create
a mirage of their own..

63. THE FALL FROM HEAVEN..

What terrible fall it was,
From glory of the highest creed,
To earth's soil, mud and dust.
From rosy hues and heavenly bliss,
Waking to earth's reality.
Words has the power to raise men,
And terribly destroy their souls,
Even the happiest of men,
Seated in heaven of contentment,
Are not immune to these,
double edged swords.
How great a sin it is,
To wound a soul with harsh words,
Such that he slips from his safe heaven,
And fall to earth and sob.
Let non of your words ever have the misfortune,
To let another man fall,
From glory high in the heavens,
To the pitiful hellfire of Earth's core.

64. MORNING IN THE WILD..

Away from the rush of the hour,
The green soothes you over..
The breeze comforts your soul,
The trees sing their rustling leaves song,
The birds fly overhead.. Free and loud,
With not a care in the world,
Other than living in their present moment...
All the little things are glorified,
And the mad human rush,
to appease egos and targets,
Seems so insignificant ..
compared to the wonderous ,
Majesty of the true wild world.

65. BIRD SONGS

Joyous songs of new dawn
Proclaiming high and loud
That this a new day, a fresh start,
And the yesterday's old and gone.
I love your happy chirping,
The grateful chorus,
The excitement in your flights..
As you hop from one branch to another,
Singing loud and clear,
Telling the whole world to wake up earlier,
And celebrate yet another days awakening..
In purest joy and wonder.
I love to watch you fly..
Celebrating each new day,
With an ecstatic heart,
While singing all the way..
And living each moment of life.

66. FINDING MYSELF

Its been a ride,
Long slow sometimes..
excruciatingly fast during others..
The whirlwinds of emotions,
So many revelations,
The constant modifications,
And the unending quest for perfection..
In order to find my ultimate self,
The more I travel within..
The more hidden treasures unearthed.
Its been a beautiful journey..
A never ending process,
that will only make sense,
with time as an ally,
And patience as a constant friend.